My Colorful Travels

IRELAND

A Coloring Book Adventure

Céad míle fáilte!

(Kade-mee-laa-fall-cha= a hundred thousand welcomes)

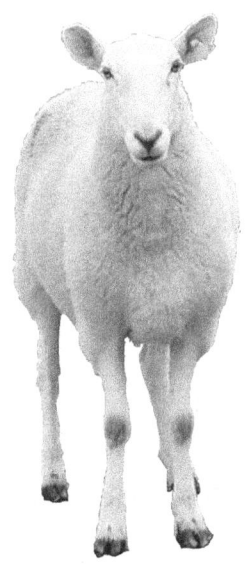

About this book

This coloring book contains thirty-five drawings of different places in Ireland. The place name of each drawing is at the bottom of each page and a brief explanation can be found alphabetically in the back of this book.

How to use this book

First choose your art medium, or how you would like to color your sketch. I like to use colored pencils; this gives you the option to layer colors for more color variation, use shading & highlighting techniques, and add shadows. If you choose, for example, fine tipped colored markers, use a piece of paper to keep the pages separate as the colors may bleed through to the next page. I have listed several coloring techniques on the next page over. There is also a blank page provided so you can test your colors and experiment with the different coloring techniques I have suggested.

Happy Coloring!

My Colorful Travels

Coloring Techniques

You can bring your sketch to life and create a unique piece of artwork by using various coloring techniques. Here are several basic techniques you could use:

Hatching - Involves drawing a series of parallel lines in one direction only. The lines can be close together, or apart. The direction of the lines can be diagonal, horizontal or vertical. This technique gives texture to a drawing.

Cross Hatching - Involves drawing a series of lines in one direction (hatching), and then drawing another series of lines in another direction on top of the first set of lines. This technique adds tonal or shading effects.

Back-and-forth stroke - This method involves using your color in back-and-forth strokes to create a solid color. It is the easiest method to use if you have a large area to color.

Stippling - Uses a series of small dots or dashes to fill in an area. You can create different effects according to the size of the dot, and also the density and placement of the dots. Stippling is another method of shading and can be used to create similar patterns to those found in nature.

Layering - Layering is the combining of two different colors together to create a new color. When layering, first use the lighter of the two colors and then add the darker color on top. Use even strokes and light to medium pressure.

Shadows - You can create shadows by first adding a light layer of black to an area before blending in a different color on top of the black.

Shading/Highlighting - This will add depth to your sketch and is very easy to do. Simply alter the pressure of your pencil or pen to make an area lighter or darker.

Burnishing (with colored pencils) - Similar to highlighting, you begin in one direction with hard pressure strokes and gradually lessen the pressure as you move your colored pencil, ending with lighter strokes. Then you take a pencil erasure or a blender pencil and start either on the light or dark end, blending the color strokes together. This creates a smoother transition between the two shades and adds a polished finish.

Use this page to test your colors and different coloring techniques.

Adare Manor

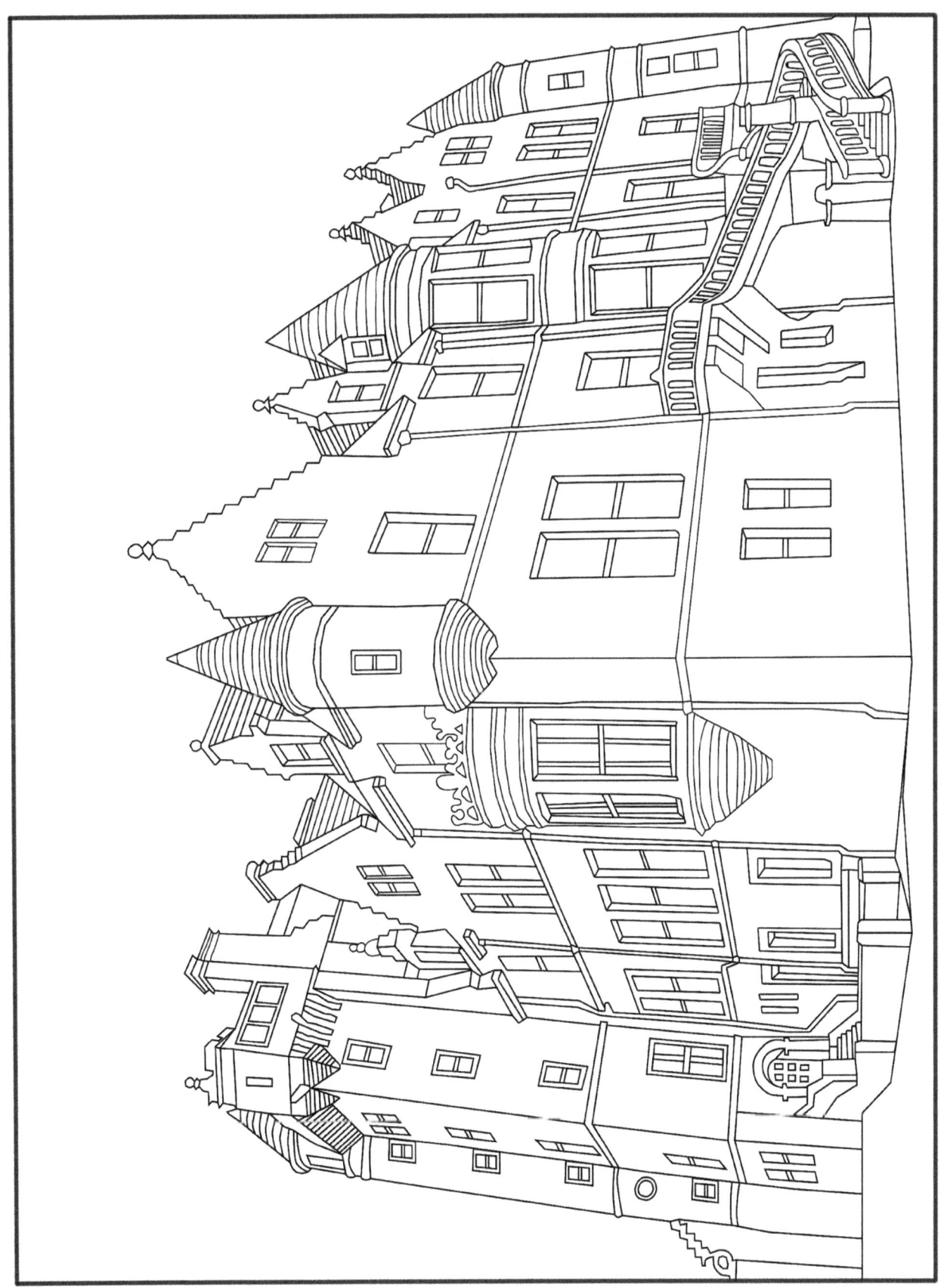

Belfast Castle

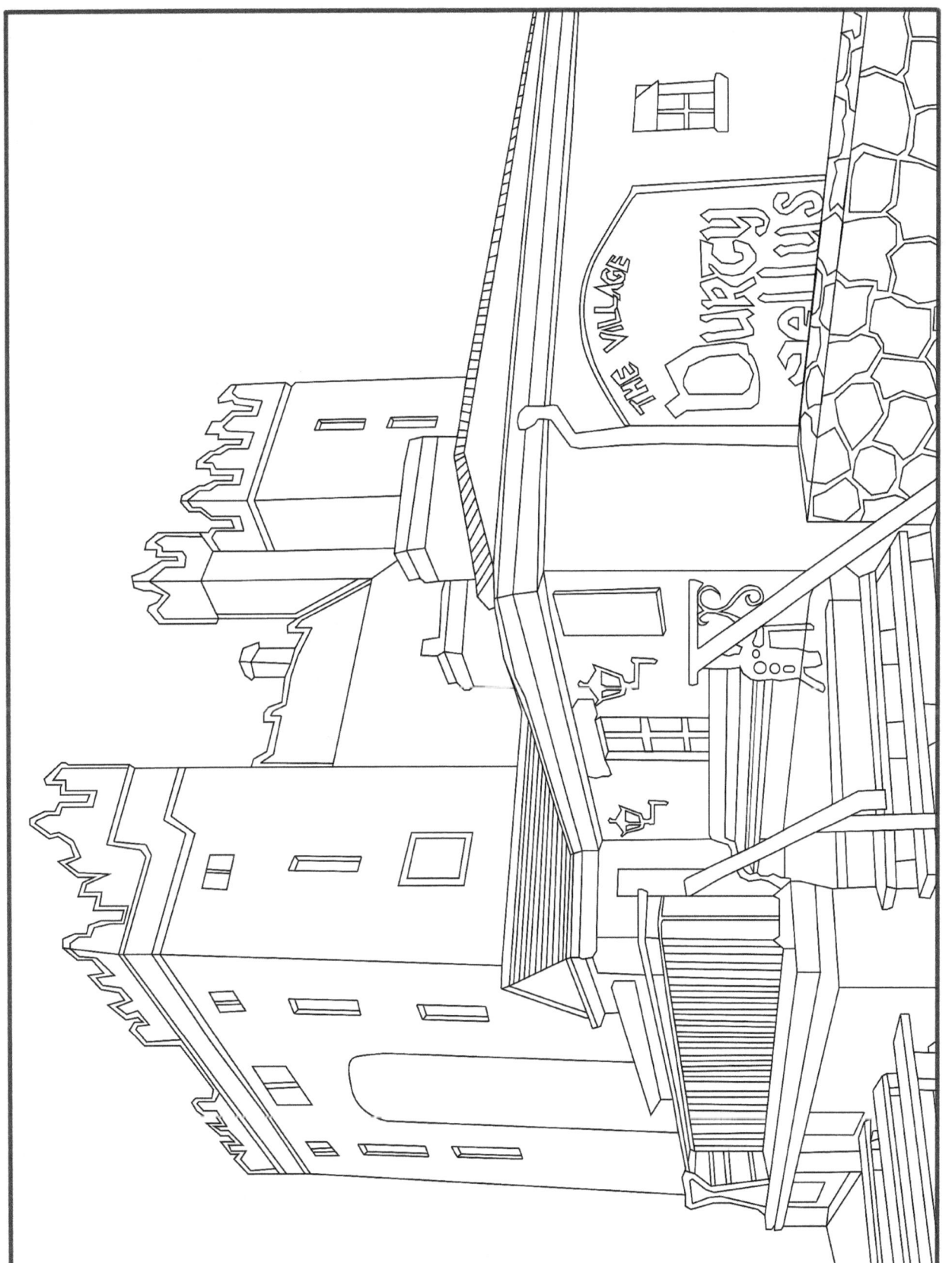

Bunratty Castle & Folk Park

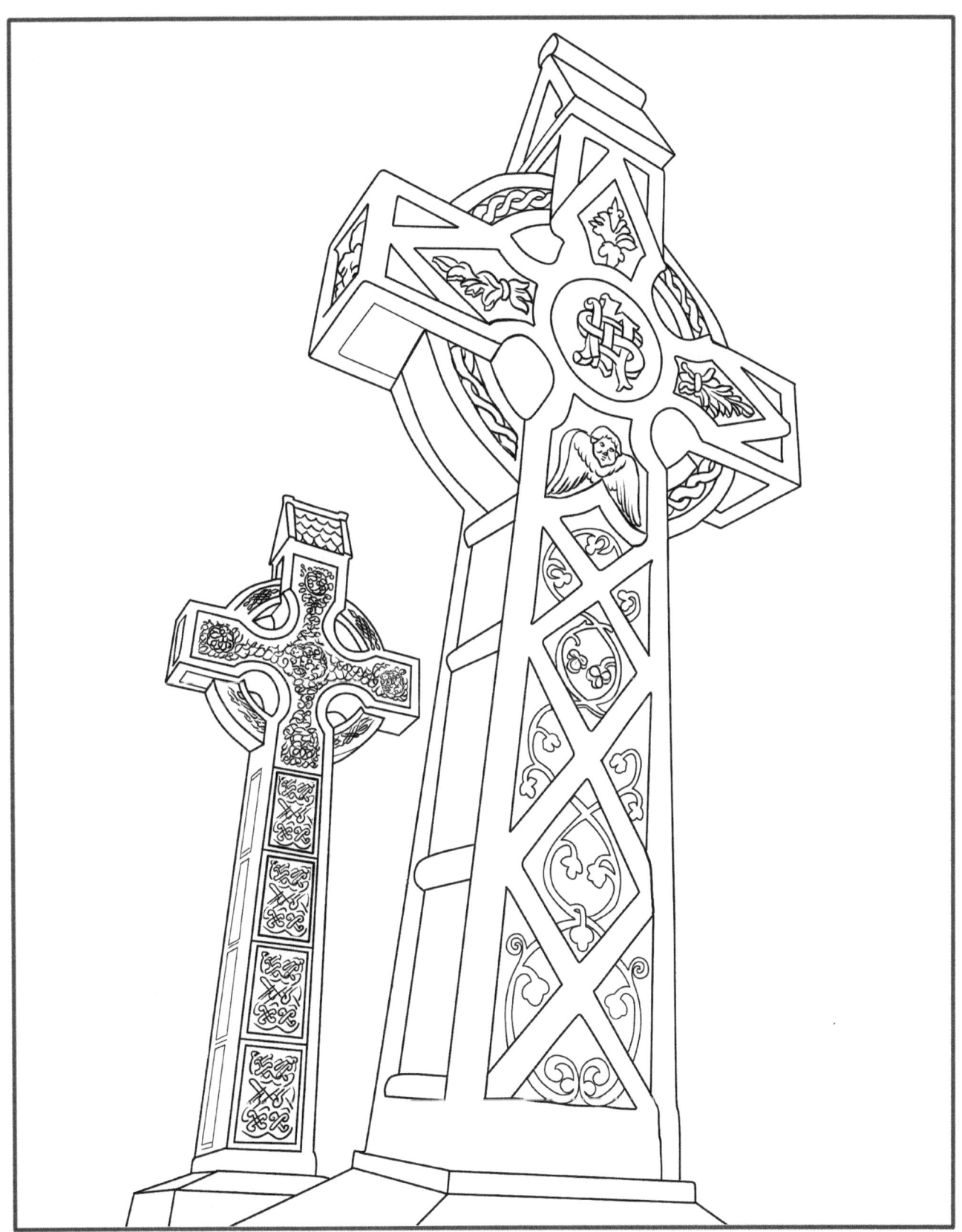

Celtic Cross

Christ Church Cathedral

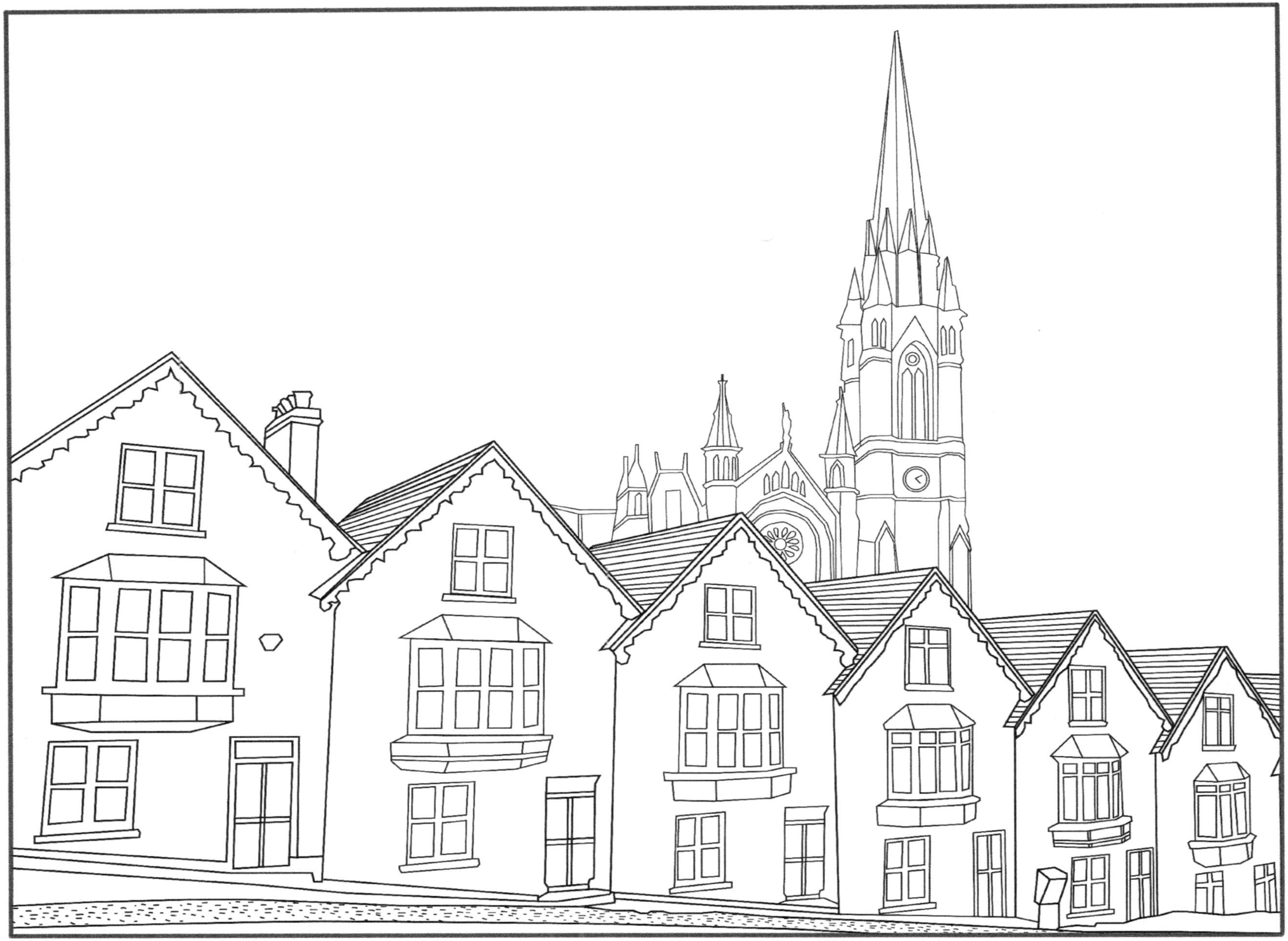

Cobh

Cottage Window

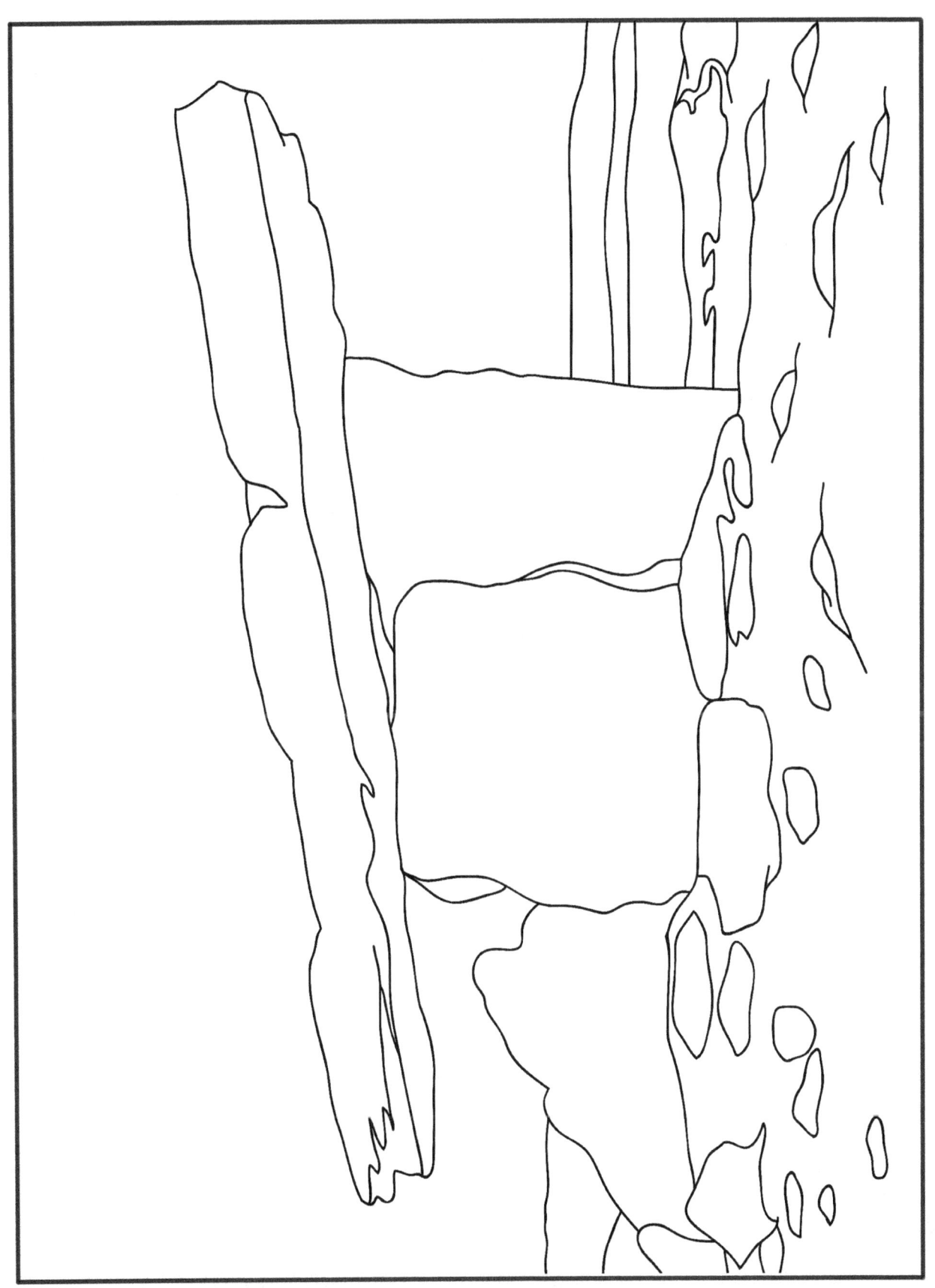

Dolmen

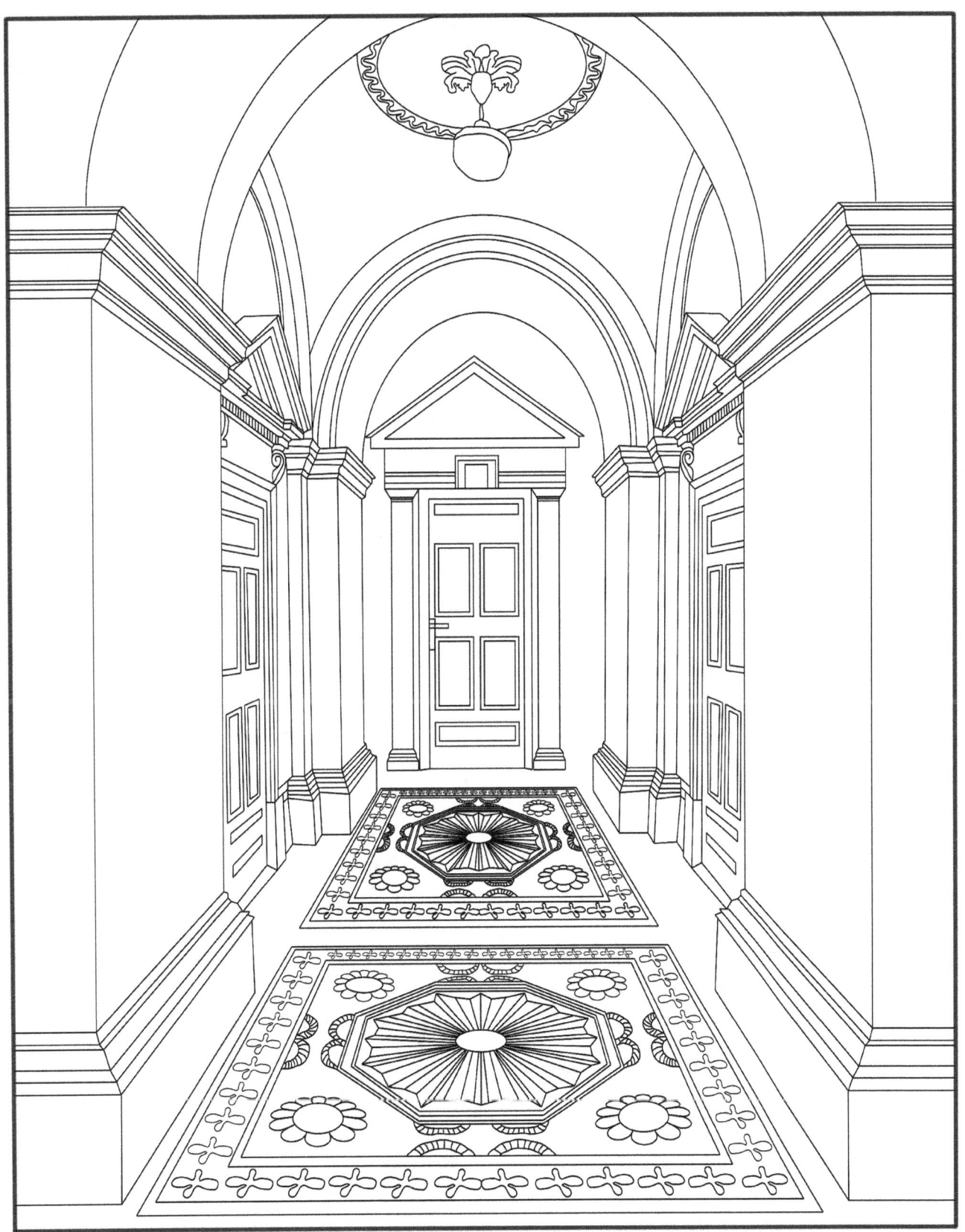

Dublin Castle

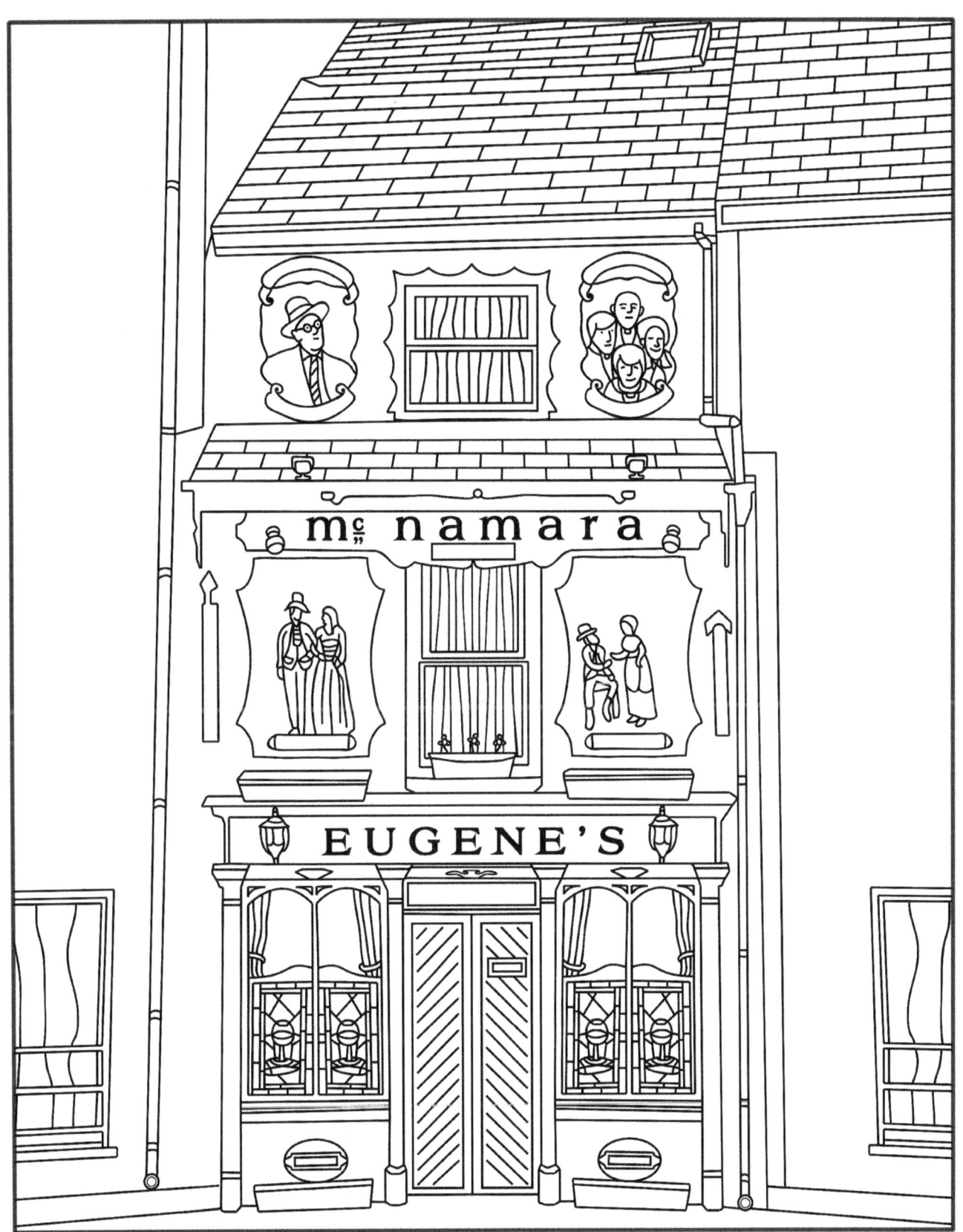

Ennistymon

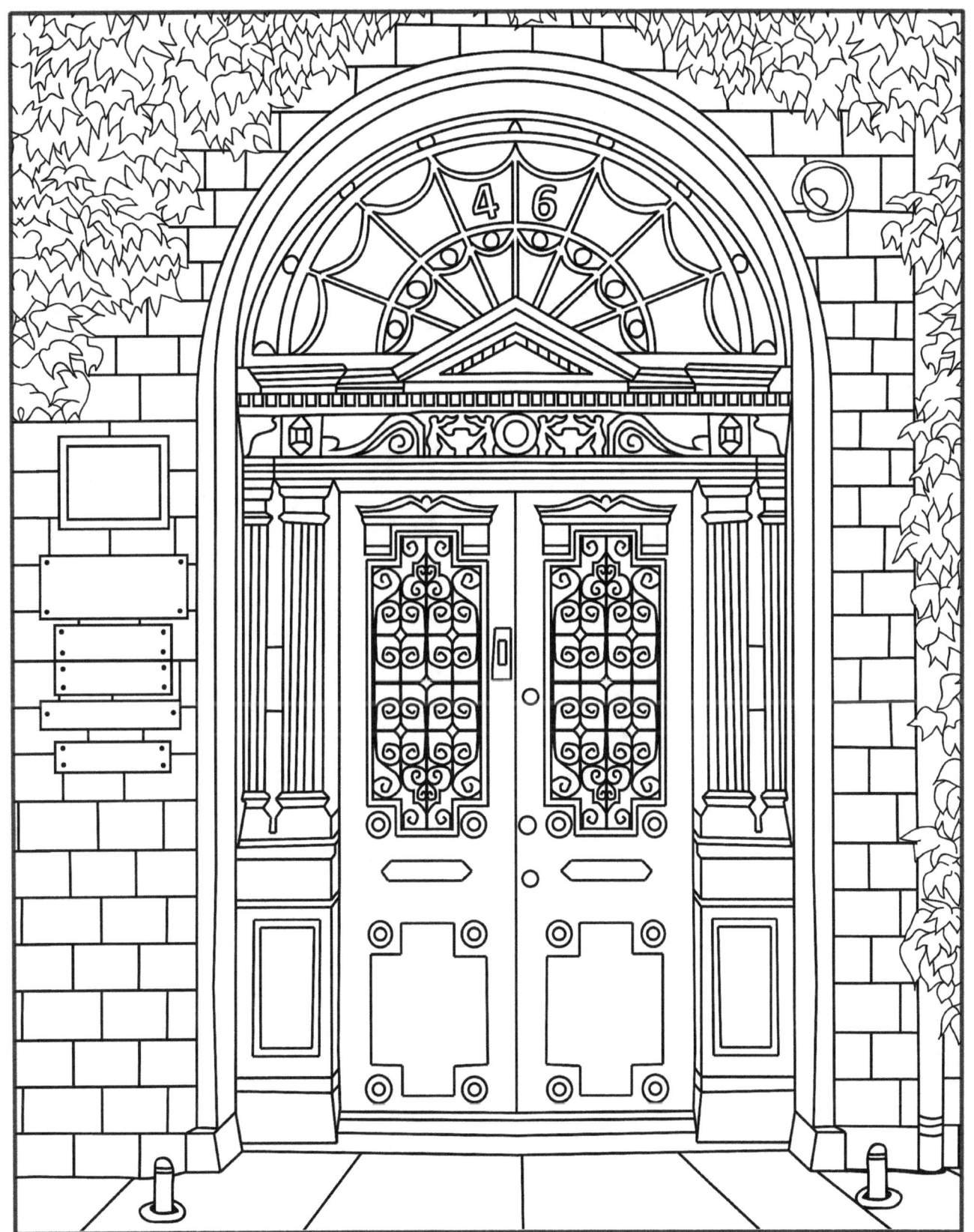

Fitzwilliam Square

Gaiety Theater

Galway Bay

Georgian Doors

Giants Causeway

Glendalough

Greyhound Pub

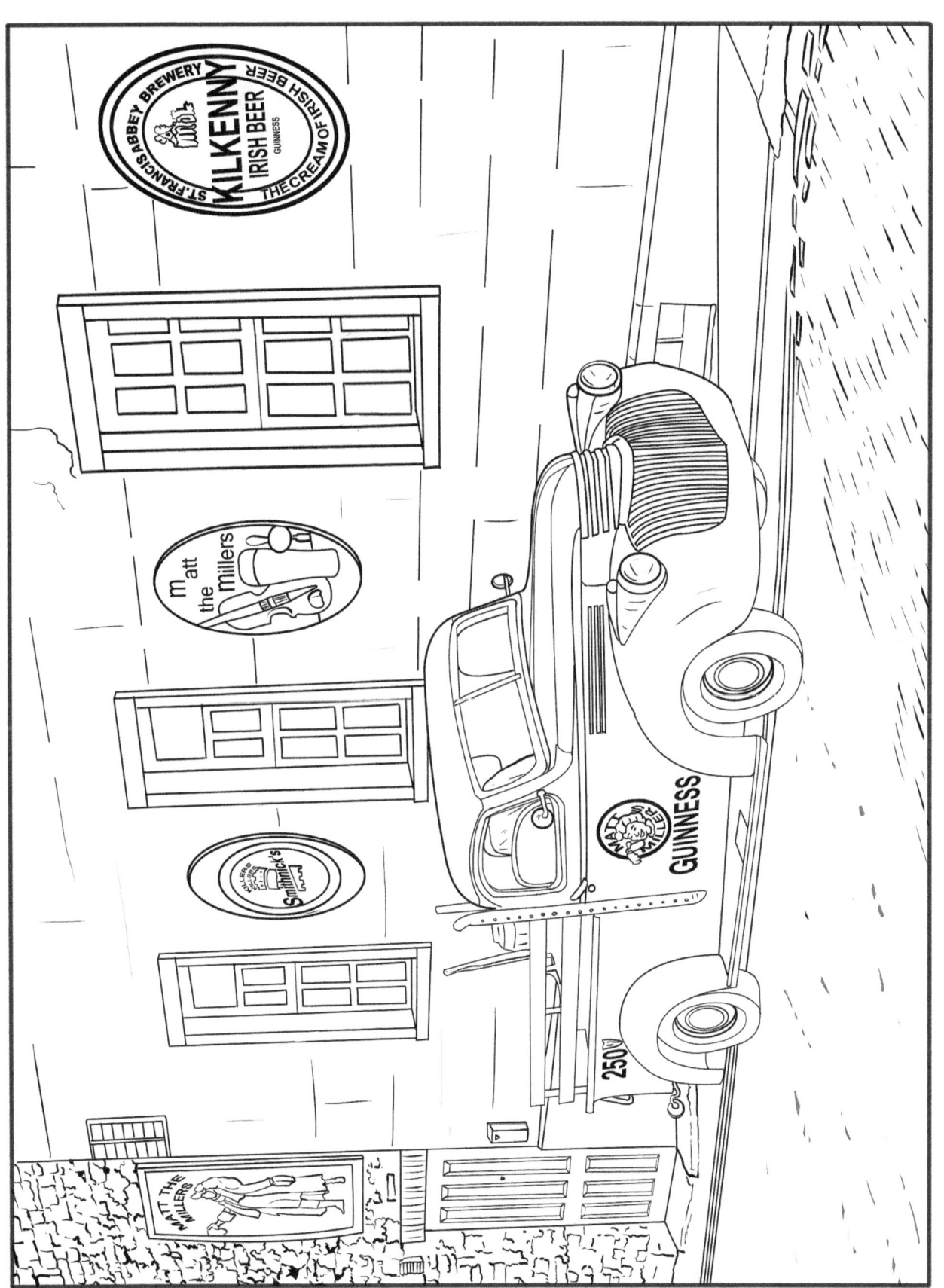

Guinness

Ha'Penny Bridge

Irish Village

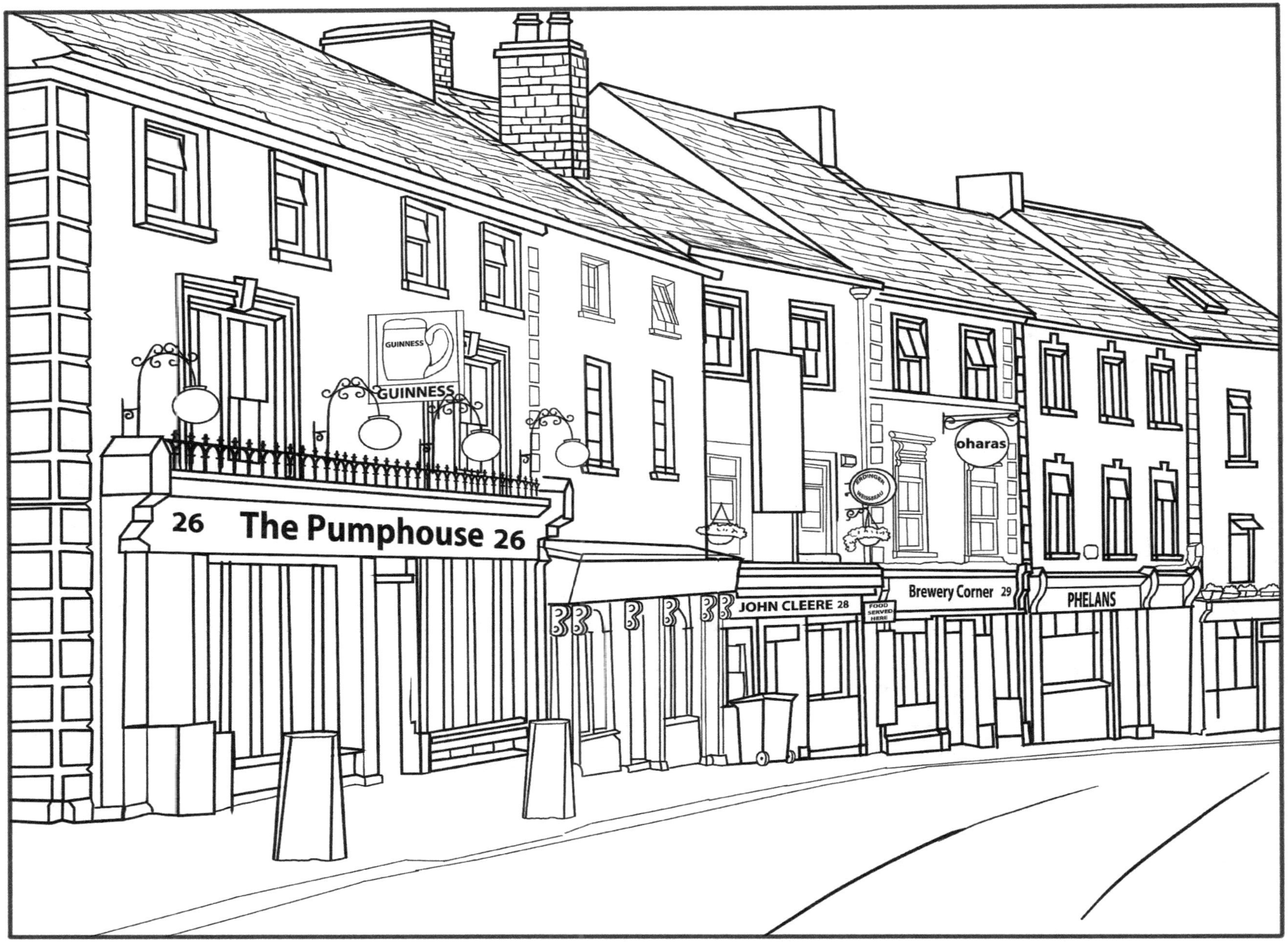

oharas

PHELANS

Brewery Corner 29

FOOD SERVED HERE

JOHN CLEERE 28

GUINNESS

GUINNESS

26 The Pumphouse 26

Kilkenny

Killarney

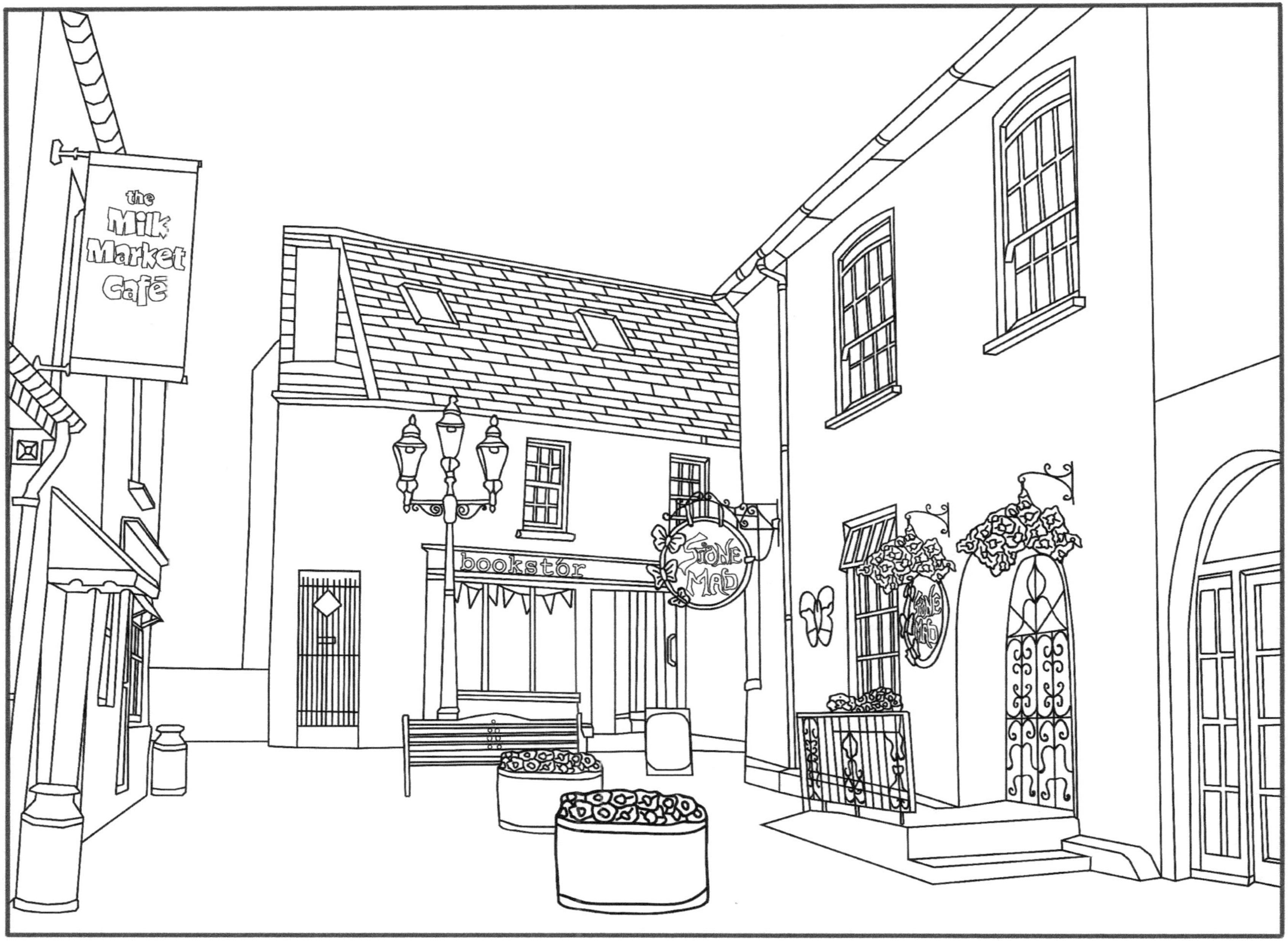

the MILK Market Cafe

bookstór

STONE MAD

Kinsale

Kylemore Abbey

Lahinch Promenade

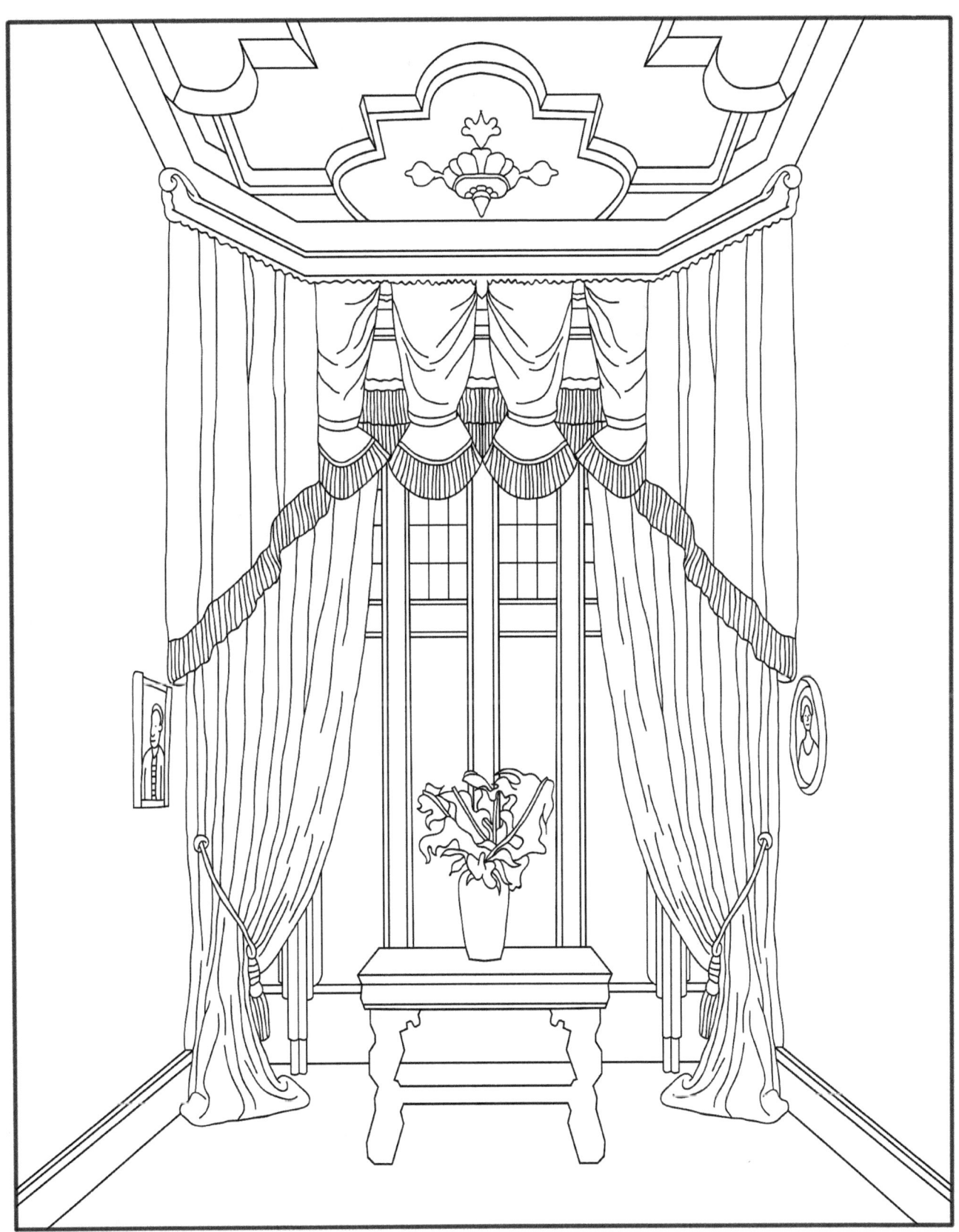

Muckross House

O'Brien's Tower

Oliver St. John Gogarty

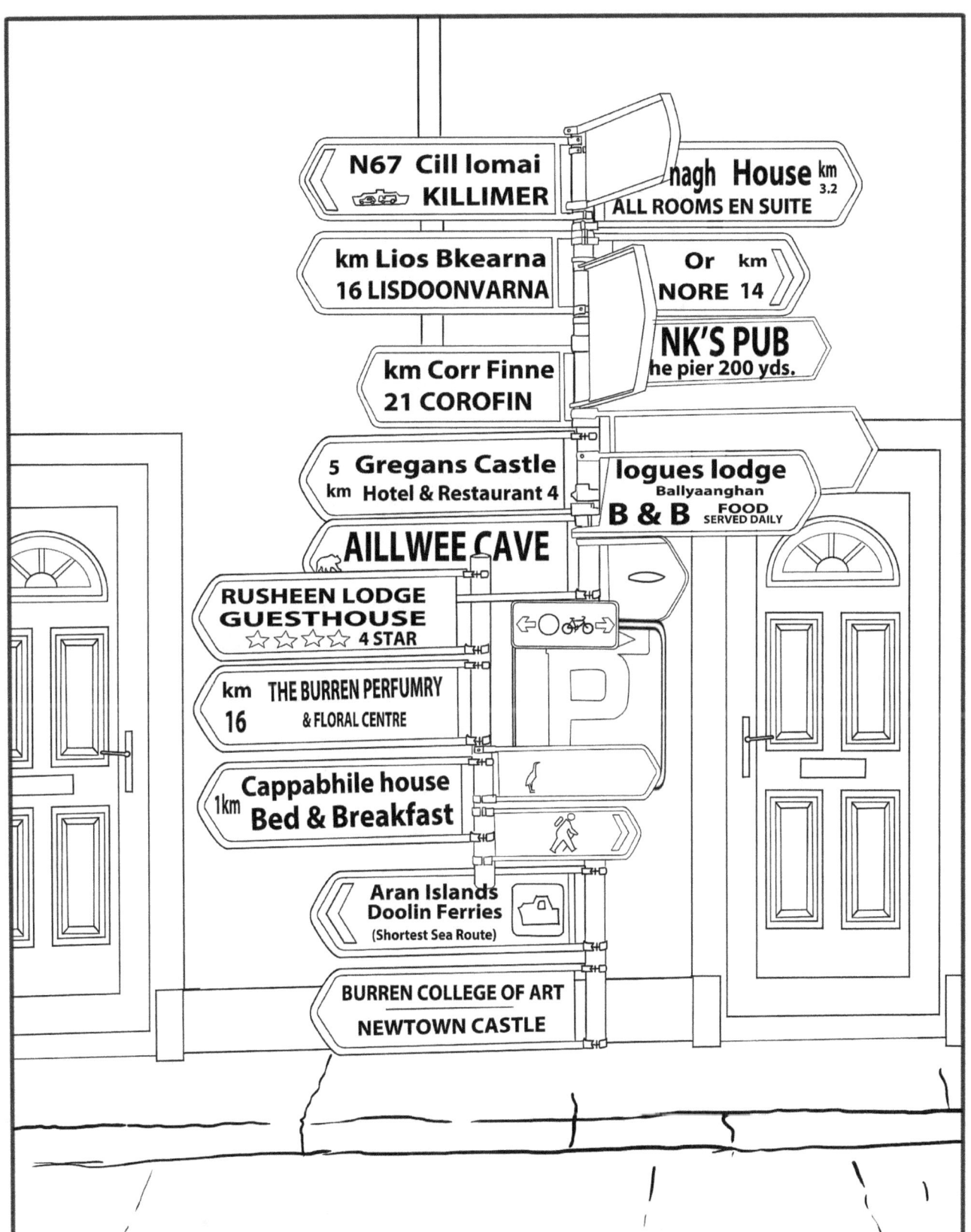

Signposts

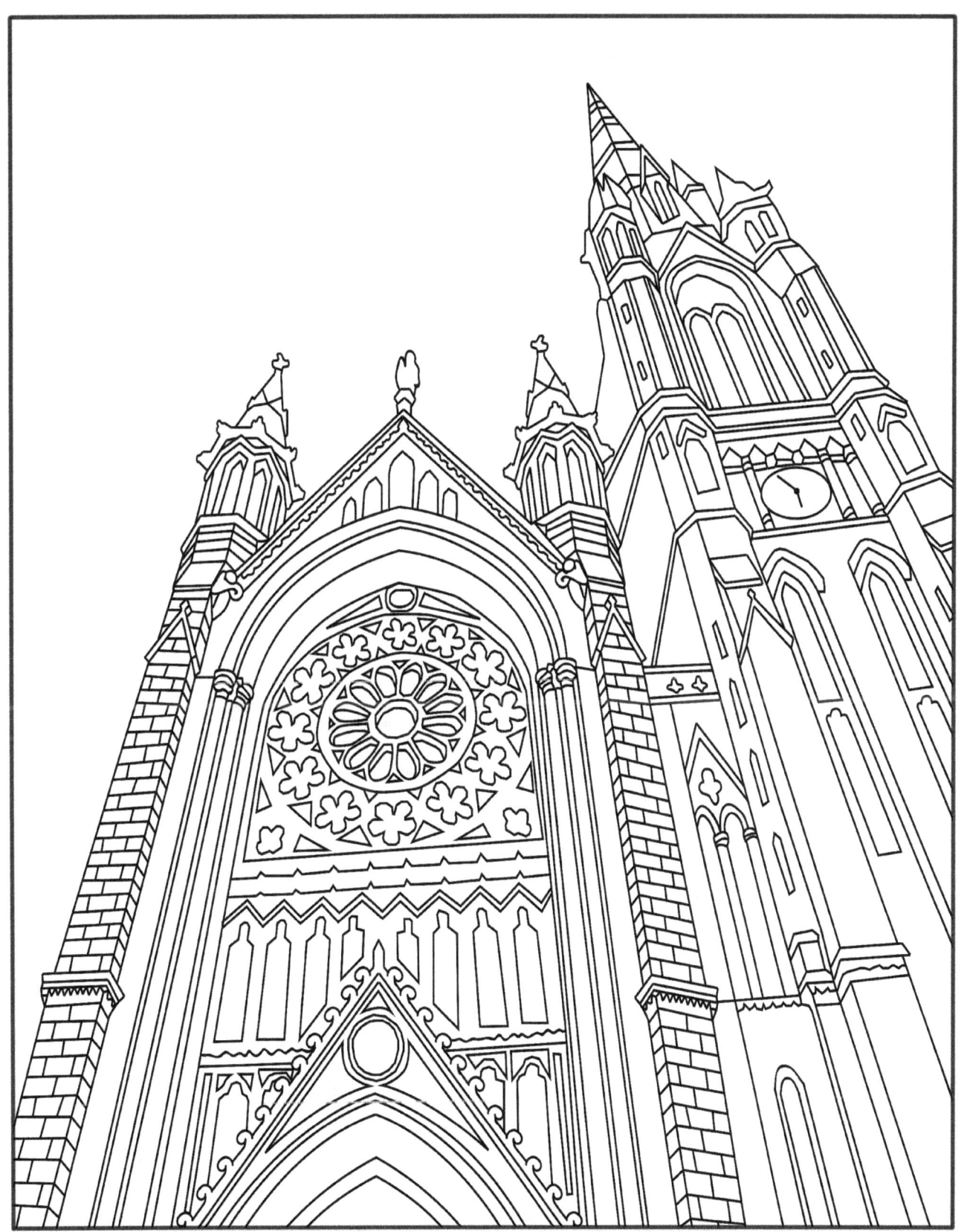

St. Colman's Cathedral

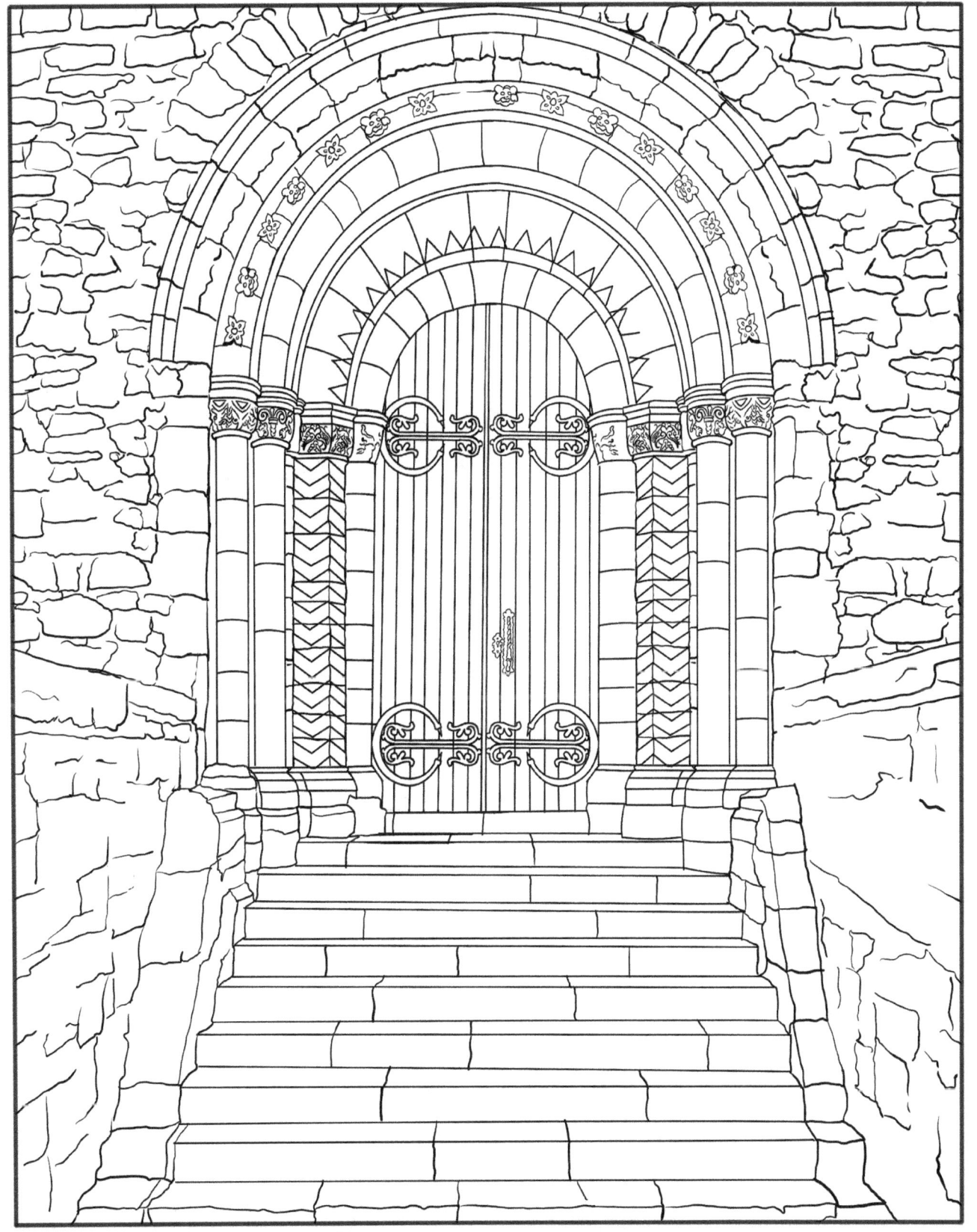

St. Mary's Cathedral

Temple Bar

Thatched Roof Cottage

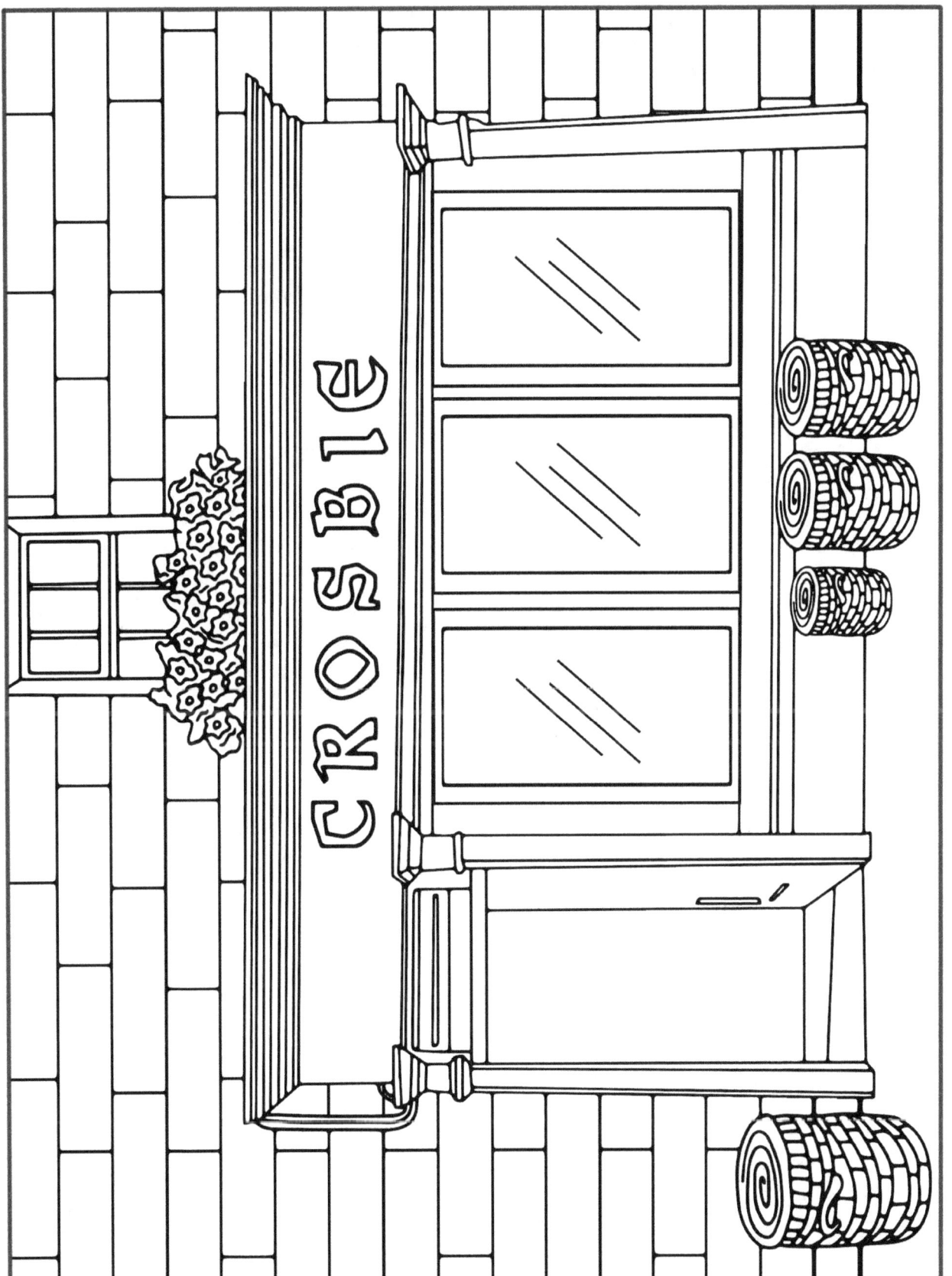

Traditional Storefront

Trinity College Library

Definitions for each drawing are listed alphabetically below:

Adare Manor is a 5* hotel and golf resort located in Adare Village, one of Ireland's prettiest villages. Adare is a designated heritage town and is located in County Limerick.

Belfast Castle was built during the 12th century and was originally located in what is today Belfast city centre. It burned down in the early 18th century and was rebuilt on an elevated site overlooking the city.

Bunratty Castle & Folk Park Bunratty Castle is an authentic 15th century medieval castle located in County Clare. The Folk Park is a living recreation of a typical Irish village during 19th century Ireland.

Celtic Cross Irish legend says that the Celtic cross was introduced to Ireland by St. Patrick. The circle is meant to be symbolic of the sun.

Christ Church Cathedral is one of Dublin's most popular tourist attractions and also contains a medieval crypt.

Cobh (pronounced 'cove') is a town located along the south coast of County Cork. It is often referred to as the 'Rainbow Town' due to its colorful houses. Cobh was the departure point for many Irish who emigrated to North America during the 19th & 20th centuries.

Cottage Window Images of picturesque Irish cottage windows often adorn postcards calendars and placemats.

Dolmen are thought to be prehistoric tombs or burial grounds.

Dublin Castle is a historical Irish government building, which was once the headquarters of the British Administration. It is open to the public.

Ennistymon is the main market town in north Clare and was once known for its traditional shop fronts.

Fitzwilliam Square in Dublin is a small private park-like area that was developed in the early 19th century; it is surrounded by Georgian houses.

Gaiety Theatre The Gaiety Theatre is located in the heart of Dublin and has been open for musical and dramatic performances since 1871. It has housed performances from people such as Julie Andrews, Joan Rivers, and Pavarotti.

Galway Bay is located along the west coast of Ireland. The Galway Hooker, a traditional type of fishing boat can be found here.

Georgian Doors can be seen on Georgian townhouses in Georgian Squares in Dublin. The doors are often brightly colored and in the past were symbolic of upper-class society.

Giants Causeway is located in County Antrim, Northern Ireland and is the result of an ancient volcanic eruption. Legend says that the columns are the remains of a causeway built by a giant.

Glendalough is located in Wicklow Mountains National Park. It is the location of one of Ireland's earliest monastic settlements.

Greyhound Pub The Greyhound Pub is one of Ireland's oldest pubs, dating back to the 17th century. It is located in picturesque Kinsale, Co. Cork.

Guinness has been brewed in Ireland since the mid-18th century.

Ha' Penny Bridge is a pedestrian bridge that crosses the River Liffey in Dublin city. It was originally constructed in the early 19th century.

Irish Village Ireland is dotted with small quaint villages, some of them quite picturesque.

Kilkenny Town is a medieval town located in the southeast. There are many heritage attractions here including Kilkenny Castle which was built in the 12th century.

Killarney Town is located in County Kerry and is also a stop along the Ring of Kerry.

Kinsale is a picturesque seaside village located in County Cork. It is known as the gourmet capital of Ireland due to its many restaurants that serve gourmet food.

Kylemore Abbey is located in Connemara, County Galway. It is a Benedictine monastery which was founded in 1920. The Abbey and its grounds are open to the public.

Lahinch Promenade The Lahinch Prom follows the coastline along Lahinch Beach. In recent years surfing has become a major attraction in Lahinch.

Muckross House is a mansion built in 1843. It is located near the Lakes of Killarney in County Kerry. Both the gardens and the house are open to the public.

O'Brien's Tower sits at the highest point of the Cliffs of Moher, which are the steepest cliffs in Ireland and stretch for five miles along the County Clare Coast.

Oliver St. John Gogarty is a hostel, restaurant and bar. It is located in Temple Bar, Dublin, and is a popular venue for 'trad' music.

Signposts This is a typical road sign in rural Ireland. Road signs in Ireland are bilingual (English & Irish) and are shown in kilometers.

St. Colman's Cathedral is a Roman Catholic Cathedral which overlooks the town of Cobh and Cork Harbor. It is open to general viewing by the public.

St. Mary's Cathedral is located in the Medieval Quarter of Limerick City. It was founded in the 12th century and is one of the oldest buildings in Limerick. It is still used as a daily place of worship and is open to the public for unguided tours.

Temple Bar is an area located in Dublin city. It has a lively nightlife along with many popular bars and restaurants.

Thatched Roof Cottage Thatching was a trade, which was usually passed from father to son. There are very few thatched cottages left in Ireland today, as thatching has to be replaced often and is expensive. Thatched cottages are most likely to be seen in picturesque villages.

Traditional Storefronts can be seen dotted around the towns and villages of Ireland.

Trinity College Trinity College is located in Dublin city centre. It was founded during the 16th century and is one of Ireland's oldest and most prestigious universities. It houses the Book of Kells, which can be viewed by the public. Notable alumni include Oscar Wilde and Bram Stoker.